CLAIRE

BEN

ELLIE

If I Ran for PRESIDENT

MARCO

SAM

ASHLEY

Catherine Stier

ILLUSTRATED BY Lynne Avril

SCHOLASTIC INC.
New York Toronto London Auckland Sydney
Mexico City New Delhi Hong Kong Buenos Aires

To those who cheer me on: Randy and my parents, Ron and Barb Beadle.—C.S.

For Ellie and Ben, future presidents, with love.—L.A.

Thanks to Michael Chaney of the New Hampshire Political Library, Concord, New Hampshire.

ISBN-13: 978-0-545-11133-1
ISBN-10: 0-545-11133-1

12 11 10 9 8 7 6 5 4 3 8 9 10 11 12 13/0

Printed in the U.S.A. 40

First Scholastic printing, September 2008

The design is by Carol Gildar.

It's fun to imagine running for the highest office in the land—and maybe becoming president of the United States of America. After all, the president is famous, makes lots of important decisions, and lives in a really cool mansion.

There are rules written in our Constitution about who can be president. A person must be thirty-five years old, so a kid really couldn't be president. Also, a person running for president must be a citizen who was born in the United States and has lived here for at least fourteen years. That's it! You can be president if you are a man or a woman. You can be president whether your parents were born in the United States or anywhere else in the world.

When citizens vote in November every four years, they are not voting directly for president and vice-president even though they mark their candidates' names on the ballot. They are voting for a group of people from their state called *electors*. In December, the electors cast their states' official votes (called *electoral votes*) for president and vice-president. The formal announcement of the winners is not until January, but usually it's clear on election night in November who has won.

Each elector votes for the candidates who won the people's vote (called the *popular vote*) in his or her state. Each state has a set number of electors, equal to the number of its senators and representatives in Congress. Altogether, there are 538 electors (including 3 for Washington, D.C., although it is not a state). When a candidate has received 270 electoral votes, he or she has won the presidential or vice-presidential election. This complicated system, which we call the *electoral college*, is outlined in the Constitution.

Running for president is surely an exhausting but exciting time for a candidate. And who knows? Perhaps someday *you* will "toss your hat in the ring" to run for president of the United States of America!

It would be great to run for president of the United States!

If I ran for president, I'd hope the people of the United States would choose me for a very important job—the job of leading our country.

And I'd hope to follow in the footsteps of past presidents such as:
George Washington, our first president,
Thomas Jefferson,
Theodore Roosevelt,
and Abraham Lincoln.

I'd have to think carefully about my decision to run for president. I would want to know how my family felt about it, too.

Then I'd ask myself: "Am I the best person for the job? Am I ready to work VERY, VERY, VERY hard for my country? Do lots of people believe in me, and will they help me run for office?"

If I could answer yes to all those questions, then I'd declare my candidacy. That means I'd announce I was interested in the job of president of the United States.

If I ran for president, I'd run a campaign to let voters learn all about me. People who thought I would be a good president would donate money or time to help. I'd hire people to work on my campaign, too.

Campaigns can make a candidate famous! Soon my name or face would appear on signs,

buttons,

bumper stickers,

and T-shirts!

I'd even star in television commercials.

If I ran for president, I'd work with my political party—that's a group of people who share the same beliefs about how the country should be governed. They support candidates who uphold those ideas. The two major parties are the Democratic party (their symbol is a donkey) and the Republican party (their symbol is an elephant). There are other parties, too, called "third parties."

But people besides me would want to be president. The Republican and Democratic parties must choose whom they'll support in the election. In some states, like Iowa, the parties each hold meetings called caucuses (KAW-kuhs-uhs), where members pick their favorite candidate. In most states, party members hold an election called a primary.

Caucuses and primaries show which candidates are popular with voters and who might have the best chance of being elected president.

The first primary is held in New Hampshire, in the winter before the presidential election. I'd be sure to visit there—but I'd have to bundle up!

In the summer before the election, the political parties announce their candidate for president. The major parties make this announcement at meetings called conventions. Each state sends delegates to the convention. Delegates vote for the candidate who was most popular in their state.

A convention looks like a big celebration, full of cheering and chanting, balloons and confetti. Millions of Americans watch the excitement on TV.

By the time of the convention, everyone usually knows which candidate will be chosen, but the delegates still hold a vote.

If my party chose me to run for president, I'd make a speech to get everyone excited about helping me win. I'd tell the American people about my platform—my plans and ideas for our country. My running mate would make a speech, too. That's the person who'd be my vice-president if I became president.

If I ran for president, I'd be invited to debate with other presidential candidates. A person called a moderator would ask us questions. People across the country would listen carefully to our answers.

Reporters would ask me questions, too, about my life, my family—even my kitten, Sassy.

They'd print old photographs of me in newspapers and magazines, like the snapshot of me in my superhero costume, or my baby picture when I still wore diapers!

If I ran for president, I would travel the country to meet lots of people. I'd have my own campaign bus or airplane to take me from place to place. Inside there'd be comfy seats, perfect for checking out the news, writing speeches, and thinking about how to solve the nation's problems.

I'd take naps, too—I'd need the extra rest!

I'd work hard and be very busy! All in one week, I might share cereal with kindergartners in California,

crunch corn with farmers in Kansas,

. . . and have dinner in Delaware, where I'd order the Blue Plate Special with apple pie and a large strawberry milkshake. After all that food, I might not feel too well! Still, I'd have to smile and talk with the people I met.

Presidential candidates make lots of speeches, shake hands—and cuddle babies.

Finally, in November, Election Day would arrive. If I ran for president, I'd be nervous and excited!

On Election Day, millions of voters from across the country go to their polling places to "cast their ballots." That's another way to say that they vote.

VOTE HE

In our country, people vote in private. No one but you knows how you voted, but I know I'd choose my favorite candidate—me!

MARCO
for

Once the voting is finished, officials count up the ballots. Then comes the announcement on television, radio, in the newspapers, and on the Internet. People everywhere find out who will be the next president of the United States.

I'd stay up late and keep my fingers crossed.

If I ran for president and lost, the people who worked so hard on my campaign would be disappointed. I'd be disappointed, too! Still, I'd be proud that I had taken part in a free and fair election. I'd make a telephone call to offer my best wishes and my support to the winner—our next president!

But if I won . . . WOW!

On January 20th, I'd say the words of the oath of office and be sworn in as president. On that day, my Inauguration Day, there'd be a parade and a fancy ball!

Then I'd move into the White House in Washington, D.C., to begin my four-year term as the president of the United States of America.

And what would I do when I became president?

Well, that's another story.